M

ACCESS TO SHAKESPEARE

The Tragedy of
Romeo
and Juliet

A Facing-pages Translation into Contemporary English

Manual for

ACCESS TO SHAKESPEARE

The Tragedy of
Romeo
and Juliet

A Facing-pages Translation into Contemporary English

Jonnie Patricia Mobley, Ph.D.
Drama Department
Cuesta College
San Luis Obispo, California

Lorenz Educational Publishers
P.O. Box 146340, Chicago, IL 60614-6340

Cover border taken from the First Folio (1623)

Cover design by Tamada Brown Design, Chicago

Interior design and typesetting by David Corona Design, Dubuque

Published by Lorenz Educational Publishers. © 1999 by Lorenz Educational Publishers. PO Box 146340, Chicago, IL 60614-6340. All rights reserved. No part of this book may be reproduced, stored in a retrieval system, or transmitted in any form or by any means without the prior permission of Lorenz Educational Publishers.

ISBN: 1-885564-03-1

Library of Congress Card Catalog Number: 94-78187

Manufactured in the United States of America.

03 04 05 06 5 4 3

Contents

INTRODUCING SHAKESPEARE

There is an aura of unreality about the plays of Shakespeare, and students feel this, although they may not be able to express their reactions precisely. They may say that Shakespeare's language is "too flowery" or that people in real life don't talk the way these characters do. And this is true. The people one meets in real life are not nearly as articulate as the characters in Shakespeare. It would probably be unbearable if the people one met at the bank and the supermarket, in school or during meetings spoke unrelievedly in the style of the great poets.

Shakespeare's characters lack the foggy-mindedness found in everyday life; they are concentrated and fully in command of their verbal resources. Shakespeare's is a world in which the brain and the heart and the tongue are directly connected. It's perhaps a world that doesn't exist, but what an interesting world it is, one in which people have fully realized their potential—for good and for evil. To have imagined such a world and to have put it on paper is Shakespeare's achievement. And it is why he is read and performed today.

Making Shakespeare's world accessible to students is the reason for this edition of *Romeo and Juliet*, a facing-pages translation with the original text on the left-hand side and a translation into contemporary English on the right. The translation of *Romeo and Juliet* is not meant to take the place of the original. After all, a translation is by its very nature a shadow of the original. This translation is an alternative to the notes usually included in modern editions. In many cases these notes interfere with the reading of the play. Whether alongside or below the original text, they break the rhythm of reading and frequently force the reader to turn back to an earlier page or jump ahead to a later one. Having a translation that runs parallel to the original, line for line, allows the reader to move easily from Elizabethan to contemporary English and back again. It's simply a better way to introduce Shakespeare.

Also, this translation is suitable for performance, where no notes are available to the audience. Admittedly, a well-directed and well-acted production can do much to clarify Shakespeare's language. And yet, there will be numerous references and lines whose meanings are not accessible on a first hearing. What, for instance, does Juliet mean when she says, "I'll stay the circumstance"?

ABOUT THIS TRANSLATION

Since 1807, when Charles and Mary Lamb published *Tales from Shakespeare,* adaptations of Shakespeare's plays have attempted, more or less successfully, to broaden the audience for these plays—or perhaps, to restore to Shakespeare the full audience he had known in the seventeenth century. These days prose paraphrases of the original are offered to students. Insofar as they succeed, these paraphrases offer a kind of literal rendering of the original, largely stripped of metaphor and poetry. To read them by themselves, without reference to the original, would make you wonder why Shakespeare is still popular.

The translation in this edition aims to retain the feel and the rhythm of the original, but at the same time to be immediately comprehensible to modern audiences and readers, so that they can experience Shakespeare in much the same way the Elizabethans did. That means preserving the sound and the spirit of the original.

Here, for example is a passage taken from the first act of *Romeo and Juliet.* The Count Paris is asking to marry Juliet and is pressing Juliet's father for his consent. Capulet protests that his daughter is still too young to be married, but Paris insists many girls younger than Juliet are already married and happy mothers. Capulet responds:

> And too soon marred are those so early made.
> Earth hath swallowed all my hopes but she,
> She is the hopeful lady of my earth.
> But woo her, gentle Paris, get her heart;
> My will to her consent is but a part.
> An she agree, within her scope of choice
> Lies my consent and fair according voice.

The first two lines are clear from what has gone before, but the trouble begins in line three with the word *hopeful.* It is not Juliet who is hopeful. It is Capulet, her father, for whom Juliet represents his hope for the future of his family. The word *fair* in the last line might be interpreted now as meaning Capulet is being fair-minded in the matter or even that his voice is *fair,* meaning "pleasant to hear." However, Elizabethan audiences would take *fair* here to mean Capulet's full or complete agreement.

To be effective and authentic, a translation into contemporary English should not only be immediately clear, but should have the ring of Shakespeare. The original and the modified parts should meld so seamlessly that, if you did not have the original at hand, you might think you were reading it:

And too soon ruined are those so early made.
Earth has swallowed all my hopes but her;
This lady's all the hope I have on earth.
But court her, gentle Paris, win her heart;
My will is but a part of her consent.
If she agrees, within her scope of choice
Lies my consent and full approving voice.

Here, for comparison, is another approach to translating Shakespeare. Although clear to a modern reader, it does not have the feel and the sound of Shakespeare.

Early married, early marred, I think.
All my other children are dead.
She is all the hope I have in this world.
But go ahead and try to win her heart, gentle Paris;
My wishes are second to hers in this.
If she agrees,
My own consent will follow.

This second translation is contemporary, not only in vocabulary, but in sound and style. It is easy to read, but it lacks the spirit of Shakespeare's work.

LINE COUNTS

Scholars of Shakespeare, following the tradition of the *Globe* edition, number the lines of verse. When they find two short lines in a row, as often happens when speakers in a play change, they count these two short lines as one. Similarly, when a line is too long to fit in the column and has to be run over, scholars count these two lines of type as one line of verse. As the British scholar G.B. Harrison explains it:

The Folio text sometimes prints short lines of verse. Editors have often joined them to make complete blank-verse lines, rearranging the rest of the speech. Shakespeare sometimes began a blank-verse speech with a half-line. This irritated editors, who shift the lines up to make them look better, until they come to some line that cannot be shifted. Then they leave it as a broken line and start again.

Consistency breaks down completely when it comes to counting lines of prose. With prose, the lines are simply numbered as they occur on the page. These methods of lineation, as it is called, have several advantages for scholars, but they can be confusing to students. To them, a line means a line of type and not a line of verse. So, if you are using a conventional text, and you ask students to look at line 18, that line could be the seventeenth line of type down from the beginning of the scene, or the nineteenth.

In this edition of *Romeo and Juliet,* every line of type is counted, short or runover, and every fifth line is numbered in the margin. Scene descriptions and stage directions are, of course, excluded from the count. With this system, you can be sure that you and your students are looking at the same lines.

SOURCE OF THE PLAY

The basic love story of Juliet and her Romeo was well known in Europe during the fifteenth and sixteenth centuries through several versions then in circulation. In England, the poet Arthur Brooke used a French source to create his poem of 3,020 lines, *The Tragicall Historye of Romeus and Juliet,* published in 1562, more than thirty years before the first performance of Shakespeare's play. Many elements of the play also occur in several Italian short stories of the time. William Painter includes one such story in his *The Palace of Pleasure* (1567). This and the Brooke poem were available to Shakespeare, and he follows the poem closely, making it his primary source.

Brooke has given some account of seeing a stage play of the story before Shakespeare's appeared, but there is no existing text. Whether or not there was such a play and no matter how helpful a source Brooke's poem may have been, Shakespeare made the story completely his own, inventing new characters, developing others, compressing the action to a dramatic length, and providing a lyrical intensity to the highly emotional tragedy.

SHAKESPEARE'S LIFE

No one knows exactly when William Shakespeare was born. What we know is that he was baptized on April 26, 1564, in the Holy Trinity Church in Stratford-upon-Avon, a small town about 100 miles from London. He was the third child of John and Mary Shakespeare. He probably attended, beginning at age four or five, the King's New School in Stratford. The school was one of the so-called grammar schools, established to teach young men to read and write and, after two years, to study Latin grammar and literature. Since the records of the school have not survived, it cannot be proven that Shakespeare was actually enrolled there. There is a record, however, in 1582 of Shakespeare's marriage to Anne Hathaway. He was eighteen at the time and she twenty-six. Their first child, Susanna, was born in 1583, and twins, Judith and Hamnet, two years later.

Between then and 1592, Shakespeare left Stratford and established himself in the world of London theatre. In that year the playwright Robert Greene published a book in which he attacked a certain actor who had the audacity to write blank-verse plays. This actor, "an upstart crow," was "in his own conceit the only Shake-scene in a country." The actor had aroused Greene's ire by successfully competing against university-educated dramatists like Greene himself.

Also in 1592, Shakespeare became a published poet with his narrative poem *Venus and Adonis*. The following year he published *The Rape of Lucrece*, another poem, and both were dedicated to the Earl of Southampton, who may have been Shakespeare's patron.

When the London theatres reopened in 1594, after having been closed to curb the spread of the plague, Shakespeare resumed his dual career as actor and dramatist. By now he was also a shareholder in his company, the Lord Chamberlain's Men, later named the King's Men. In 1599 Shakespeare's company built their own theatre on the other side of the Thames River, across from London. Shakespeare apparently prospered and invested his income in real estate in London and Stratford. Sometime between 1610 and 1613, he returned to Stratford and retired.

He died on April 23, 1616, and was buried two days later within the chancel of Holy Trinity Church. The inscription on his stone in Holy Trinity Church reads as follows:

Good friend, for Jesus' sake, forbear
To dig the dust enclosed here.
Blest be the man that spares these stones
And cursed be he who moves my bones.

Several years after his death, in 1623, two members of Shakespeare's company, John Heminge and Henry Condell, collected his plays and published them in what has become known as the First Folio. Previous to this, Shakespeare's plays were sometimes published individually as quartos. (A quarto is a sheet of paper folded in quarters, or fours, and a folio is a sheet of paper folded in half, or twos. A quarto yielded eight pages of type, and a folio, two. In effect, a quarto was a small book containing a single play; a folio was a larger book containing a collection of plays.)

Shakespeare's last direct descendant, his granddaughter, Elizabeth Hall, died in 1670.

SHAKESPEARE'S LANGUAGE

Shakespeare's language does present problems for modern readers. After all, four centuries separate us from him. During this time words have acquired new meanings. For example, a *competitor*, in Shakespeare's time, referred to a partner or to an associate. *To let* meant "to hinder," *passing* meant "surpassing," and *by and by* meant "immediately." Some words Shakespeare used have dropped from the language altogether, and sentence structures have become less fluid. But the problems represented by these changes can be resolved.

First of all, most of the words that Shakespeare used are still current. In this translation, for those words whose meanings have changed and for those no longer in the language, modern equivalents are used. For a small number of words—chiefly, names of places and biblical and mythological characters—a glossary, chronologically arranged, can be found on page 247 of the text of the play. Another glossary, alphabetically arranged, will be found in the manual on page 41.

The meaning of words is one problem. The position of words is another. Today, the order of words in declarative sentences is almost fixed. First comes the subject, then the verb, and finally, if there is one, the object. In Shakespeare's time, the order of words, particularly in poetic drama was more fluid. Shakespeare has Juliet say:

But all this I did know before.

Whereas we would usually arrange the words in this order:

But I knew all this before.

Earlier in the play, Paris says:

Of honorable reckoning are you both.

We would probably say:

You both are of honorable reckoning.

This does not mean that Shakespeare never uses words in what we consider normal order. As often as not, he does. Here, for instance, are Romeo and a servant in conversation:

SERVANT   But, I pray, can you read anything you see?
ROMEO   Ay, if I know the letters and the language.

When Shakespeare inverts the order of words, he does so for a variety of reasons—to create a rhythm, to emphasize a word, to achieve a rhyme. Whether a play is in verse, as most of this play is, or in prose, it is still written in sentences.

And this means that, despite the order, all the words needed to make complete sentences are there. If your students are puzzled by a sentence, tell them to first look for the subject and then try rearranging the words in the order they would normally use. It takes a little practice, but they will be surprised how quickly they acquire the skill.

Shakespeare sometimes separates sentence parts—subject and verb, for example—that would normally be run together. Here are some lines spoken by Benvolio, describing the encounter between Romeo and Tybalt:

> All this uttered
> With gentle breath, calm look, knees humbly bowed,
> Could not take truce with the unruly spleen
> Of Tybalt, deaf to peace . . . .

Between the subject *this* and the verb *could not take* comes a compound prepositional phrase that interrupts the normal sequence. Again, have your students look for the subject and then the verb and put the two together. The rearranged sentence, though clear, will probably not be as rhythmical as Shakespeare's.

SHAKESPEARE'S THEATRE

When most people think of a theatre building, they picture the proscenium arch auditorium, but, of course, there are other types: the thrust stage, the black box (a room designated for performances and painted or draped entirely in black), and the "found space" of a converted cafeteria or campus quad. The closest to Shakespeare's theatre, the "Wooden O" of the Globe Theatre, is the present-day arena theatre where the audience surrounds the stage. The Globe, where most of Shakespeare's plays were originally produced, was a circular or polygonal wooden structure of galleries surrounding an open courtyard area. In the middle of this courtyard was a covered wooden platform. Immediately in front of this platform was the area designated the "pit" (much later it became our modern orchestra pit, and the seats sold as orchestra seats) where the groundlings stood. These were the rowdy, uneducated rabble who paid a small fee to attend a play, and the low comedy elements in Shakespeare's plays were directed toward them. Patrons who could afford it paid more and sat in the surrounding galleries or even on the stage itself.

Most of the play's action took place on the platform itself. At the rear of the platform was a curtained alcove which could be used to represent an inner room or a tomb, depending on the needs of the play. On the second level, above the alcove, the area, uncurtained, could serve to represent a bed chamber or balcony.

The third level of this back wall could serve as yet another setting but was more often where the musicians sat.

The fourth level was closed off from the audience, and from there came the sound effects such as the bird song indicated in *Romeo and Juliet*. The platform had trap doors. Right and left of the mainstage area were tiring, short for retiring, rooms where the actors could dress.

There were no curtains to conceal the mainstage from the audience, so plays flowed from scene to scene without interruption, or perhaps with only the slightest pause or brief musical interlude to indicate a change of time or place.

Because the Globe was open to the air, performances could utilize the natural illumination of daylight, although torches were also used. The whole structure of the Globe (and other theatres that imitated it) reminds us of the yards of inns where the first traveling companies of medieval actors often played.

The elaborately constructed and painted scenery that one often sees in a modern production of Shakespeare was missing from the original productions. Companies were content to suggest or symbolize a setting. Several cutouts of trees could suggest an orchard; torches and benches, Capulet's ballroom; and some large constructed stones, the entrance to the tomb.

There was sparing use of props, but some are documented in a list of stage properties kept by Philip Henslowe, the Elizabethan theatre magnate. The production of *Romeo and Juliet* might call for such items as a small flask and letters.

Costumes were not as lavish as in many modern productions, but the leading players were certainly dressed appropriately with swords, or in party clothes or in nightdress.

As there were no women in the theatre companies of Shakespeare's time, all the parts were played by men and by the boys who were apprentices in the company. As one looks at the cast lists for the plays, it is easy to see that the male characters outnumber the women, and for a very practical reason. However, the women's parts that do exist offer actors wonderful opportunities.

The repertory system for theatrical companies came into being with the construction of the permanent theatre building in London. In order to keep attracting an audience to their plays, the companies had to change their offerings frequently. In a two-week period a company might offer as many as ten different plays in rotation. An actor with the lead in one play would be expected to take a minor role in the next play in rotation, perhaps have a break from the third play, and again appear in a minor role for the next play, and then once again play a lead in the fifth play. As new plays were introduced into the repertoire, actors found themselves rehearsing a new play while still performing in an older one. Actors in repertory companies needed physical stamina, versatility in acting, and had to be quick studies—that is, fast at memorizing lines.

STAGE DIRECTIONS

In drama written for the modern stage, the playwright provides detailed directions for the actors—how to move and speak, what emotions to convey to an audience. In the plays of Shakespeare, stage directions are sparse. One reason for this could be that Shakespeare was a member and an owner of the company for which he wrote these plays. He was there to tell the other actors how to say a line or what gesture to use. Even so, the dialogue itself offers clues to actions and gestures. For example, in Act One Capulet breaks off his scolding of Tybalt to compliment the dancers at his party. He says:

> You're a cocky lad, aren't you?
> This behavior will harm you. I know that.
> If you disobey me then it's time—
> Oh, good dancing there, friends—you show off!

The actor playing Capulet obviously must turn from Tybalt, look to the dancers as they go by, and then turn back again to continue scolding Tybalt, although the printed text contains no such stage directions.

Remind your students that as they read, they must be alert to whom a line of dialogue is addressed. For example, Romeo and Benvolio are strolling on a street in Verona. When Benvolio asks Romeo if he is mad, Romeo answers:

> Not mad, but bound more than a madman is;
> Shut up in prison, kept without my food,
> Whipped and tormented and—

Then turning to a passing servant he says,

> Good evening, fellow.

But there is no stage direction to mark this change of address.

Again, when the Nurse returns from her meeting with Romeo, she runs on about how exhausted she is. Instead of giving Juliet her news, she says,

> Lord, how my head aches. What a headache I have!
> It pounds as if it's going to break in twenty pieces.
> My back, too. On the other side. Ah, my back, my back.

Juliet is presumably rubbing the Nurse's back, but there is no stage direction for this. Urge your students as they read to picture in the characters in their minds, visualize what they are doing, and decide who is talking to whom.

TRANSITIONS

Abrupt transitions occur fairly frequently in Shakespeare. Often, they are used simply to advance the plot. However, they also frequently reveal a psychological interplay between the characters. For example, in conversation with Benvolio, Romeo says:

> Oh me, sad hours seem long.
> Was that my father who left here so fast?

Benvolio responds to the second point first:

> It was.

But then he pursues the first matter,

> What sadness lengthens your hours, Romeo?

In this passage Benvolio shows the normal reaction of first responding to a question, but he then shows his concern for his friend by going back to Romeo's earlier statement about the sad hours.

SOLO SPEECHES

There is another difference between the plays of Shakespeare and most modern ones—the solo speeches. These are the asides and the soliloquies in which a character reveals what is on his or her mind. Contemporary dramatists seem to feel that the solo speech is artificial and unrealistic. Oddly enough, modern novelists frequently use a variety of the solo speech. Some critics feel that this convention has given the novel extra power and depth, allowing writers to probe deeply into the motives of their characters. One thing is certain—Shakespeare's plays without the solo speeches would not be as powerful as they are.

TEACHING SUGGESTIONS

There are several ways in which this edition of *Romeo and Juliet* can be used with students, but perhaps the most effective is to assign a long scene or several short scenes in the translation for reading as homework. Then, in going over this material in class, use the original. This way much valuable time can be saved. Students no longer have to struggle with understanding the basic story, and you can devote your time to providing insights and in-depth appreciation of the play.

For some students, of course, the original text will still represent a formidable obstacle. In those cases, you may want to use the translation as the basis of classroom presentation with carefully selected passages from the original to illustrate the points you are making. The great advantage of this edition is its flexibility in a variety of teaching situations.

ADDITIONAL TEACHING SUGGESTIONS

Because this is a play rather than a novel or short story with descriptive passages to provide exposition, you will probably want to discuss with your students the motivations of the various characters, their relationships with each other, and even the effect of time and place on them.

1. A kind of theatre game many directors use to help their actors understand the complexities of the characters in a drama like *Romeo and Juliet* is called "Collage." To adapt it to classroom use, assign each student a character in *Romeo and Juliet*. It doesn't matter if more than one student has the same character as long as they don't confer. Each student must choose a color for the background—using colored paper or quickly coloring in a background. The color, of course, represents the character as the student perceives him or her. Most students are aware of the theories of colors and how they affect us, but even without such formal knowledge students are generally adept at choosing a color that suggests what their character is like.

   Next, using magazines or newspapers or even simple drawings, each student creates a collage of objects, shapes, and scenery that together present all the student understands about the character he or she has been assigned. The collages are shared, one by one, with the class, and the total effect of each is discussed. If two students have the same character, the result should not be a debate over who is *right* but, rather, if there are differences of opinion between the two, why did each make those particular choices of interpretation?

2. One of the elements of *Romeo and Juliet* which has been highly praised is the skill with which Shakespeare compressed the rambling time sequence of his source and made the story take place in just a few days. Nothing strains our credibility, as motivations are always clearly set forth and characters are carefully developed so that all that happens seems right within the framework established.

   To enable students to see exactly how this works, have them construct a time line for the events of the play. They can do this on scratch paper until they are satisfied they have accounted for everything and then print it out on a long strip of paper or on poster board, using a board for each day in the play's plot. Once they can look at the results, they should be impressed not only with the amount of action packed into two hours of stage time, but also with the way Shakespeare has managed the interweaving of events.

3. The universality of *Romeo and Juliet* is one of the reasons often cited for its enduring popularity. It might be difficult to locate the French, Italian, or even the English sources often given for the play, but Ovid's *Metamorphoses* is in most libraries and by reading the tale of Pyramus and Thisbe in that collection, students can see an early version of the romantic story of two star-crossed lovers. Then, after they have read *Romeo and Juliet*, they could watch a video of the filmed version of the Broadway musical *West Side Story*. Even listening to a cast recording of the songs from the show can help them see the modern parallels with Shakespeare's story.

SUMMARIES OF ACTS AND SCENES

PROLOGUE

A Speaker (Chorus) announces that this play concerns two lovers in Verona, who seem destined by fate and their feuding families to have their romance end tragically. The Speaker, who summarizes the story in a sonnet, also promises to make clear in the performance any detail that may puzzle the audience.

ACT ONE

Scene 1

Rather than gradually introduce the idea of two quarreling families, the action immediately plunges the audience into the problem, as we see even the servants of the two households are eager to pick a fight with the other side. Benvolio, a Montague, tries to calm things down, but Tybalt, a Capulet, wants to fight. (Benvolio's name in Italian means "I wish well.") The citizens of Verona protest the rioting, but the head of each household rushes into the argument, despite the protests of their wives. Prince Escalus restores order and warns that death will be the punishment for any more fighting between the Montagues and the Capulets. Romeo, a Montague, arrives, and he and Benvolio discuss Romeo's melancholy over his unrequited love for Rosaline.

Scene 2

At the Capulet house, Count Paris is urging Juliet's father to permit him to marry his daughter. Capulet protests that she is too young and asks Paris to wait a while longer. Capulet plans a party for the evening and sends a servant out to invite the people on a list. The servant can't read and so asks a passerby, Romeo as fate would have it, to read the list to him. In gratitude, the servant invites Romeo to the party—providing he is not a Montague. Romeo and Benvolio decide to attend anyway, and Benvolio points out that the party will provide many lovely ladies to compare to Rosaline.

Scene 3

Lady Capulet sends the Nurse, Juliet's attendant, to bring Juliet to her. The Nurse rambles on about Juliet when she was a girl, providing some exposition about Juliet before we meet her. Juliet's mother tells her of Paris' proposal, but Juliet does not show much enthusiasm for the prospect. At fourteen she is of marriage-able age in that time, but as the Nurse's commentary has shown us, she is unsophisticated and not eager to be married.

Scene 4

Outside the Capulet home, Romeo and some friends, all in party masks, gather and plan a dance for the festivities. Romeo is gloomy and fearful that something bad will happen, or at least begin, at the party. His friends try to cheer him up, in particular Mercutio, who tells him a story about Mab, Queen of the Fairies, who causes disturbing dreams for many. Finally Romeo agrees to go in with the others.

Scene 5

The masked group is greeted by Capulet, who reminisces with a cousin about their last masked ball many years ago. Romeo sees Juliet and falls instantly in love. Tybalt recognizes his voice and is about to attack Romeo, but Capulet scolds him for making a scene at a party. He tells Tybalt that Romeo is well behaved and has a good reputation and that it is his—Capulet's—house and party, so Tybalt is to behave or leave. Meanwhile, Romeo and Juliet talk briefly and exchange a kiss. As he leaves, Romeo inquires about Juliet and finds to his dismay that she is the daughter of Capulet. Juliet inquires after Romeo and learns to her dismay that he is a Montague. The tender exchange between the two is written in the form of a sonnet and uses the comparison between pilgrims touching hands with saints and lovers touching lips.

ACT TWO

Prologue

The Speaker tells us that Romeo has forgotten Rosaline in his newfound love for Juliet. He cautions, however, that their way will be difficult because of their families' feud. Still, the Speaker says, like all lovers, they will find a way to meet secretly.

Scene 1

Romeo, unwilling to leave the home of his beloved, hangs around the grounds, hoping for a glimpse of her. His friends Benvolio and Mercutio hunt for him, and Mercutio in particular makes jokes and comments at Romeo's expense to tease him out of hiding.

Scene 2

Juliet, at her bedroom window, talking aloud to herself about her feelings for Romeo, is overheard by him. Encouraged by what he hears, Romeo moves out into her view and they each acknowledge their love for one another. They agree to marry and very reluctantly part. Juliet is to send a messenger to Romeo in the morning to learn of the wedding arrangements he will have made by then. Romeo leaves to consult his priest.

Scene 3

The priest, Friar Lawrence, is gathering herbs and flowers and speculating on their uses and abuses. This foreshadows the later use of some sleep-inducing herbal potion in the plot to save Juliet from an undesirable marriage, and the fatal use of some poisonous herb by Romeo. When Romeo appears there so early in the morning, the friar fears he has spent the night with Rosaline and is therefore greatly surprised to learn that Romeo has a new love and wants to be married immediately. The friar scolds him for being so fickle, but agrees that such a marriage might be a means of reconciling the two warring families. Many critics have pointed out that Romeo was merely playing the game, then dictated by fashion, of unrequited love with Rosaline, but that he is quick to recognize real love when he meets Juliet.

Scene 4

Romeo's friends Benvolio and Mercutio discuss his being out all night and decide that Tybalt has probably challenged him to a duel as a result of the ball the night before—he not only crashed the party but he was seen talking to Tybalt's cousin Juliet. Mercutio makes fun of Tybalt's French affectations and his skill at sword fighting. When Romeo arrives, Mercutio teases him about the famous beauties of legend who must pale before the charms of Romeo's love Rosaline. Romeo joins in the joking but does not tell his friends that his love is now Juliet. The Nurse arrives and is insulted by Mercutio's crude humor, but she manages to speak privately with Romeo and learns of the wedding arrangements he has made. Juliet is to ask to go to confession that afternoon, and there at Friar Lawrence's monk's cell Romeo and she will be married. The Nurse is to return later to get a rope ladder that Romeo will use to climb to Juliet's chamber that night. The way Romeo enters into the battle of wits with his friends shows him to have put off the melancholy he displayed earlier: he is now happy and hopeful.

Scene 5

Juliet eagerly awaits the news from the Nurse who delays and delays by grumbling about how tired and sore she is from running all over town on Juliet's behalf. This is good-natured teasing but agonizing for Juliet. Finally, though, the Nurse explains the plans for the marriage that afternoon.

Scene 6

Romeo awaits Juliet at Friar Lawrence's cell. When she arrives, they are married. The friar worries aloud about such sudden passion, fearing it may have a sudden end, but he continues to hope the union will help to reunite the Montagues and the Capulets.

ACT THREE

Scene 1

On a street in Verona, Benvolio senses trouble coming, and when Tybalt and his friends appear, they seem ready for a fight. Benvolio tries to keep the peace but Mercutio responds to Tybalt's insults with some of his own. When Romeo arrives, Tybalt turns his wrath on him. Romeo answers politely, though, and hints that he has good reason to be friendly with Capulets. Mercutio is ashamed of his friend's soft answers and decides to fight Tybalt himself. In trying to break up the fight, Romeo unknowingly allows Tybalt to get in a thrust at Mercutio, who is stabbed and dies cursing both families for their feud. Tybalt runs away but then returns and forces Romeo to fight and kill him. Romeo, at Benvolio's urging, flies the scene as the Prince arrives with the elder Montagues and Capulets. Benvolio describes all that has gone on. The Prince, seeing that Tybalt provoked his own death by killing Mercutio, decides that Romeo will not be executed, but that he must be banished from Verona as an example to others who insist on fighting. This scene, about the same length as the love scene at Juliet's balcony, shows the other side of the coin and may be called a hate scene. Certainly it spoils any chance for happiness the two lovers had, since Romeo's banishment means that the couple cannot announce their marriage, and Juliet will be vulnerable to any plans her father may make for her to marry Paris.

Scene 2

Unaware of what has happened, Juliet awaits her bridegroom. The Nurse brings in the rope ladder by which Romeo was to climb to Juliet's room, but she also brings the dreadful news that Tybalt has been killed and Romeo banished. In her usual rambling way, the Nurse first manages to confuse Juliet into thinking it is Romeo who has been killed, but on learning the truth Juliet decides that banishment is even worse. She is a little comforted by the Nurse's promise to bring Romeo there that night to say farewell. Although she is very young and somewhat bewildered by all that her wedding night may bring, she is nonetheless eager to be a wife in the physical sense.

Scene 3

Like Juliet, Romeo sees his banishment as worse than death. When Friar Lawrence attempts to comfort him with a philosophical view, Romeo threatens suicide. The Nurse arrives to explain that Juliet is in just as bad a state, and both she and the friar reproach Romeo for his lack of faith. Romeo is encouraged by the Nurse's plan for him to join Juliet that night, and he accepts the ring she has sent. The friar warns Romeo that he must leave by daylight for his exile in Mantua. If he is discovered by the change of watchmen, his sentence will be changed to death. The friar also promises to send all news of events in Verona to Romeo by messenger.

Scene 4

Old Capulet assures Paris that he will persuade Juliet to marry him. In fact, he picks the next Thursday, only three days away, for the wedding. It will be a small celebration out of respect for Tybalt's recent death. Then Capulet sends his wife to tell Juliet of the plans, hoping that this happy news will take her mind off grieving for Tybalt. Of course the news is not happy for Juliet, and it's not Tybalt, but Romeo, she is grieving for.

Scene 5

Even though Juliet tries to convince Romeo that the bird they hear singing is the nightingale, they both know it is the morning lark, and Romeo must leave for Mantua. The nurse interrupts their touching farewells with the announcement that Lady Capulet is on the way to see her daughter. When the mother arrives, she tells Juliet she is to prepare to marry Paris on Thursday. Juliet tearfully declines and angers her mother, who insists she must stop this excessive grieving for Tybalt and get on with her life. Although Juliet cleverly disguises her meaning from her mother, she manages to protest that she can marry no one unless it be Tybalt's killer. Capulet enters and adds his orders to his wife's, insisting that the marriage to Paris will take place on Thursday. After the elder Capulets leave, Juliet's Nurse tells her she might as well marry Paris; after all, he is a good man and Romeo is out of the picture now. Juliet is disgusted and angry with the Nurse for such advice but hides her feelings and decides to visit Friar Lawrence for his advice. If there is nothing else to be done, she will take her own life. This tendency by both Romeo and Juliet to threaten suicide when things go wrong may seem melodramatic, but they are both young, passionate, bewildered, and desperate. Neither confides in their parents and neither pauses to thoroughly think things out. All that helps to precipitate the tragedy.

ACT FOUR

Scene 1

Paris goes to see Friar Lawrence to arrange for his own marriage to Juliet. He tells the friar that they will marry without a formal engagement period because he and her father feel it will help Juliet to get over Tybalt's death. Juliet arrives, and she and Paris exchange pleasantries that we know to be charged with double meaning on Juliet's part as she tries to evade Paris' affections. He leaves, and she turns to Friar Lawrence with a desperate plea for some solution to her problem. She says she would rather die than marry Paris. Encouraged by her daring, the friar suggests that she take a sleep-inducing potion that will give the impression of death. There will be a funeral and entombment in the Capulet crypt. Romeo will be sent for and, when she awakens, he and Romeo will be there to rescue her from the tomb. Juliet bravely agrees to do this frightening thing in order to be reunited with Romeo. The potion the friar provides reminds us of his earlier skill with herbs, so we are hopeful for the success of this plot.

Scene 2

Juliet pleases her parents by pretending to agree to their wedding plans for her and Paris. The older Capulets are quickly caught up in these plans for the ceremony and feast to follow it. When he finds the servants all busy with the preparations, Capulet goes himself to tell Paris the happy news.

Scene 3

On Friar Lawrence's instructions, Juliet asks to be allowed to sleep alone that night, without her attending Nurse, saying that her mother will need the Nurse to help her with her preparations for the celebration. Although she tortures herself with visions of her entombment and the madness that could follow if she awakens too early in that frightening place, Juliet bravely swallows the potion and falls into a death-like sleep.

Scene 4

Early the next morning, the whole household is still at work on the preparations. The Nurse teases the master of the house by calling him "cot-quean," or one who does women's jobs, because he is so involved in all the work. He sends her off to awaken Juliet.

Scene 5

The Nurse cannot awaken Juliet and cries out that she is dead. Paris arrives and joins in the general outcry of sorrow. Even the musicians he has brought with him refuse to play a tune the servant Peter requests, feeling it would be disrespectful to the family. Friar Lawrence arrives and attempts to offer words of comfort while urging an immediate funeral and placing of Juliet in the tomb. We can imagine his relief that the plan is succeeding so far. The exchange of joking insults between Peter and the musicians that ends the scene provides comic relief and also reminds us that for Juliet this is not a sad occasion, but, rather, a means of escaping a dreaded and bigamous marriage.

ACT FIVE

Scene 1

Romeo, exiled in Mantua, has a strange dream of dying but then being brought back to life by Juliet's kisses. It has left him puzzled but happy. His servant Balthasar arrives and tells him that Juliet is dead and lies buried in her family's crypt. Romeo decides to go to Verona as soon as he can buy some poison, and then he will take his own life beside Juliet in her tomb. He remembers a poverty-stricken apothecary he saw in the town and is sure that he can be persuaded to break the law against selling poison in Mantua. Romeo is right; although the man initially makes a feeble protest, he does finally sell Romeo a flask of quick-acting poison. We wonder why Romeo doesn't know that Juliet is only asleep, waiting for his arrival to rescue her.

Scene 2

We soon find out that Friar John, who was to take a message to Romeo about the plot Friar Lawrence devised, had been unexpectedly delayed. He and a brother monk had been sealed up in a house after health officials suspected contamination from plague. Friar John still has the letter meant for Romeo. Alarmed that Juliet will soon awaken and Romeo won't be there to comfort her, Friar Lawrence gets a pickaxe and spade and prepares to rescue her himself. While health officials certainly would act in the manner indicated where there was any threat of plague, it seems that so ironic a circumstance must have been fated for the two young lovers.

Scene 3

Paris comes to the tomb to place flowers and tells his page to listen for anyone approaching. Someone does arrive, and it proves to be Romeo and Balthasar with tools for opening the crypt. Romeo sends Balthasar away, but Balthasar lingers nearby, afraid that Romeo means to kill himself there with Juliet. When Romeo breaks into the tomb, Paris accuses him of desecration. They fight, and when Paris is killed, Romeo realizes he is his rival for Juliet and so he places his body in the tomb with her. Then he bids Juliet farewell and drinks the poison he has brought. Friar Lawrence rushes in too late to prevent this, but in time to see Juliet awaken and find Romeo dead. She will not leave him, but the friar leaves to avoid the watchmen. When the poison Juliet kisses from Romeo's lips fails to kill her, she uses his dagger. The Prince, citizens of Verona, and finally the Montagues and Capulets arrive to see the two young lovers joined in death. The friar explains all that has happened, and the Prince absolves him from blame. Instead, the Prince says that the tragedy is a judgment on the two warring families and that all have been punished by it. Capulet and Montague join hands in reconciliation, and each promises to put up a statue in memory of the other's child. The Prince pronounces the last words of the play by reminding us that there never was a story of more woe than this of Juliet and Romeo.

QUESTIONS FOR DISCUSSION

ACT ONE

1. The Prologue gives away the story, even telling of the death of Romeo and Juliet. Do you think Shakespeare made a mistake by writing the Prologue?

   COMMENT: The story of Romeo and Juliet was a familiar one to the Elizabethans. They did not attend the play to see how events turned out. Marchette Chute, in *Shakespeare of London*, has written, "The Elizabethan theatre was not based on the element of surprise but on the gratification of expectations." In staging the play today, the Prologue here and in Act Two are often omitted.

2. Why do you think Shakespeare never explains how the feud between the two families began?

   COMMENT: The history is not important to our understanding of the feud because we have immediate evidence of it in the opening scene, with the brawl between the servants of the two households. The feud has infected everyone connected with the two families and now needs no more provocation than a look or a word to erupt into open fighting. It is the effect on the heirs of the original participants that concerns us in this play.

3. What irony is there in the chance encounter between Romeo and the Capulet servant?

   COMMENT: Because the servant cannot read, he asks a passerby for help in reading the list of people he has been sent to invite to Capulet's party. The passerby is Romeo, and his kind action in reading the list for the servant earns him an invitation to the party. However, it also ironically earns him his death, as he is fatally attracted to Capulet's daughter at that party.

4. Why is so much importance attached to the fact that Juliet is still rather young to be married?

   COMMENT: Her naivete helps to account for her quickness to fall in love at first sight, her haste in agreeing to marry Romeo, her gleeful participation in a secret marriage, and her quick change of mood from blaming Romeo for Tybalt's death to her defense of him.

5. Mercutio's name is close to "mercurial" and the characteristics of eloquence, shrewdness, and changeable temperament. How well does that describe him?

   COMMENT: It fits him well. His wit is displayed in all the joking among his friends; even as he is dying he manages the pun, "Ask for me tomorrow and you shall find me a grave man." He is shrewd in judging Romeo's reason for running away from his friends after Capulet's party, although he can't know that Juliet has replaced Rosaline in Romeo's affections. And Mercutio is changeable, as we see in the street scene, where he at first teases Benvolio about being quick to fight and then he is himself quick to challenge Tybalt.

6. Compare Tybalt's behavior in the street fighting scene 1 with his later behavior at the Capulet party when he hears a Montague voice.

COMMENT: He is consistent. In both cases he is quick to take offense, quick to start a fight, quick to join in an existing fight, and impatient with anyone who attempts to calm him down. It's easy to spot him as a source of trouble for Romeo.

ACT TWO

1. The Prologue speaks of the difficulties Romeo and Juliet will have to overcome. What are these?

COMMENT: As their families are sworn enemies, the two young lovers will have to find a way to meet in secret. They will not be able to tell anyone of their love and so will have no support of friends or family to see them through. Although the Nurse is aware of their marriage, she is quick to tell Juliet she will have to marry Paris if her father insists.

2. Although Mercutio has most of the lines in scene 1, what impression do we form of Benvolio?

COMMENT: He seems less of a jokester, a bit more philosophical than Mercutio, and certainly of a milder temperament. He realizes that all their calling out to Romeo and all their teasing of his lovelorn state will not bring him out if he wishes to stay hidden away.

3. The balcony scene is famous for its poetry and often done as a set piece— that is, complete in itself without context. What is there about the scene that makes it understandable to an audience even without the scenes that went before it?

COMMENT: Both the characters give an account of their falling in love, the depth of that love, and their dreams and desires for their future together. They discuss their families' mutual hatred and declare it makes no difference to their love. The scene captures the essence of the play's conflict and gives us a very romantic encounter to enjoy.

4. Instead of meeting Friar Lawrence in his monk's cell, we first find him gathering herbs and flowers. What does that foreshadow?

COMMENT: The friar's knowledge of plants will be important later, when Juliet asks for help in avoiding the marriage to Paris. We learn of his skills here so we are prepared for his solution of a sleep-inducing potion later.

5. What is there about the Nurse's manner or conduct that seems to invite the rude treatment Mercutio gives her?

COMMENT: She talks too much and probably too loudly. She dresses in a manner that provokes comment. Although she says nothing vulgar in scene 4, we have heard her vulgar or at least earthy comments previously. The line "Lady, lady, lady" that Mercutio sings as he leaves the scene is intended as his parting shot at the Nurse.

6. What comic relief is provided by the Nurse when she returns from meeting Romeo?

COMMENT: Even though she can see Juliet is anxious to hear what plans Romeo has made for their wedding, the Nurse complains about the walk to town, babbles on about Romeo's looks and manners, and finally, as Juliet runs out of patience, gives her the details she is longing for.

7. Why is the friar reluctant to marry the young couple?

COMMENT: Romeo had very recently been moaning to him about his unrequited love for Rosaline, and now he wants to marry a girl he has just met. Also, their families are enemies, so a marriage between them is bound to cause them trouble and may even cause trouble for the friar if he performs the ceremony.

ACT THREE

1. This act, unlike the previous two, has no prologue. What is the effect on the audience?

COMMENT: We have no hint about events to come, but that cannot trouble us for long, since we are immediately involved in the fight between Romeo's friends and some of the Capulets led by the quarrelsome Tybalt.

2. What causes Juliet to change abruptly from happy anticipation of her wedding night to despair?

COMMENT: The Nurse brings the news of Tybalt's death and the subsequent banishment of Romeo. In those times such an exile would mean an end to any hope of their being together. There were, of course, no telephones, no post office, no public transportation system—in short, no way for a young girl living with her parents to communicate with or visit a young man in another town without her parents' knowledge and help.

3. Romeo at Friar Lawrence's cell has despair equal to Juliet's. What manages to cheer him up?

   COMMENT: The Nurse arrives and with the friar arranges for Romeo to spend the night with Juliet. Although he is still faced with banishment, at least he will have his wedding night and that prospect manages to put off his gloom for the time being.

4. What excuse does Capulet offer for arranging such a hasty marriage for his daughter?

   COMMENT: Because Juliet is so worried about Romeo, she has been moping in her room and crying. She has allowed her family to think this grief is for the death of her cousin Tybalt, so her father says he will end her sorrow with a quick wedding, and then she will have the cheering companionship of Paris. Paris, who has wanted to marry Juliet for some time, is quick to agree to this pretext.

5. Scene 5 opens with romantic bliss and ends with a resolve to commit suicide. What has brought about this abrupt change in Juliet?

   COMMENT: At the start of the scene Romeo is still with her, and although he must depart, they have time for a tender farewell. With his departure, Lady Capulet arrives to inform her daughter that she must bend to her father's will and marry Paris in just two days. Even if she were free to marry anyone, Juliet would not want to marry Paris, and she certainly does not want to commit bigamy. If the friar cannot help her, she determines, she will take her own life.

ACT FOUR

1. What hidden message do we hear in the replies Juliet gives to Paris' attempts at romance when they meet at Friar Lawrence's cell?

   COMMENT: All her answers are meant to put him off, to avoid anything that could be perceived as encouragement. She says only that she loves the good friar. She disparages her own beauty and agrees that her face does not belong to Paris, but it does not belong to her either. This is a difficult encounter for Juliet. She must put aside her own worries and do nothing to arouse suspicion in Paris, and yet she will not allow herself to pretend affection for the count, as that would be a betrayal of Romeo.

2. How is Juliet able to pretend gladness at her proposed marriage to Paris?

   COMMENT: She knows she will not have to go through with the wedding thanks to the plan the friar devised. Also, it is much easier to pretend to give in to her father's commands than to argue with him.

3. What wild thoughts torture Juliet as she is about to drink the potion the friar gave her?

COMMENT: Not surprisingly, she is haunted by the image of awakening too early in the sealed tomb and being driven mad by the ghastly sights contained there: rotting corpses, old bones, even her cousin Tybalt's bloody body lying there. But she is brave enough to drink the potion anyway.

4. What impression of Capulet do we receive in scene 2 that is a little at odds with what we know of him from other scenes?

COMMENT: Previously we have seen him as an angry foe, a nostalgic host, and a father who insists on being obeyed by his daughter. He has even called her some ugly names in his anger at her proposed disobedience. In scene 2, however, we see him as a fond father, fussing over every detail for the wedding feast of a beloved child. He doesn't even mind being teased by the Nurse about doing women's work.

5. What is Friar Lawrence's reaction at entering the Capulet house and being greeted by news of Juliet's death?

COMMENT: The friar must act surprised. He must attend to his duty of consoling the grieving family, and in this case he scolds them for not realizing Juliet is now in a higher place than even her father's ambitions could hope for. Then, of course, he urges an immediate funeral and entombment. We know how important such actions are to his plan of having Juliet presumed dead until Romeo can arrive to rescue her.

ACT FIVE

1. Why are we as surprised as Romeo at Balthasar's news of Juliet's death?

COMMENT: We thought Romeo would know of it by now and understand it as part of the plot to reunite the lovers. We also thought that he would already be on his way to Verona to rescue Juliet. To find him still in Mantua and obviously unaware of the friar's plot is a shock.

2. How accurately has Romeo perceived the apothecary?

COMMENT: He has sized him up exactly. His poverty has reduced him to the state where he will break the law of the city by selling poison to a distraught young man who surely means to use the poison for suicide.

3. What has happened to the message that Friar Lawrence sent to Romeo concerning the potion plot?

COMMENT: His messenger, Friar John, was unable to deliver the letter. In fact, he still has it with him. A call on the sick resulted in his being suspected of contact with the plague, and so he has been under house arrest.

4. When he arrives at Juliet's tomb, why does Romeo send away his servant Balthasar?

   COMMENT: Romeo is afraid that Balthasar will realize his intention to commit suicide there beside Juliet and will try to stop him. In this, he is right, but although Balthasar is suspicious of just such an action and he stays as nearby as he dares, he still is not able to prevent Romeo's desperate action.

5. What cruel chain of events results in both lovers dying?

   COMMENT: Since she has not awakened yet when he arrives, Romeo still believes Juliet to be actually dead, not merely asleep, so he kills himself. She awakens just too late to stop him and kills herself in grief. The friar arrives just too late to explain things and prevent both deaths.

6. Upon awakening, Juliet notices the cup from which Romeo drank the poison. ("What's here? A cup in my true love's hand?") Where does the cup come from?

   COMMENT: Europeans, unlike the early Egyptians, did not provide articles of use for the dead to take with them in the afterlife. So Romeo must have brought the cup with him. Even today, most Europeans consider it bad manners to drink directly from a bottle.

7. What is the purpose of the statues the elder Montague and Capulet propose to have erected?

   COMMENT: Each statue will commemorate the other's child as a truce offering, but also the statues will serve to remind the town of what such hatred between families can cause. Furthermore, Juliet's statue will proclaim her fidelity to her husband Romeo.

STAGING *ROMEO AND JULIET*

There are four main locations in which a class might mount a production of *Romeo and Juliet*—in a proscenium arch auditorium, in an arena theatre, in a found space, or outdoors. Although some elements remain the same, each situation requires different considerations.

PROSCENIUM

In a proscenium arch auditorium, the audience usually expects a box set, rendered in as representational a manner as possible. Such a stage often allows for such tricks as trap doors to allow characters to disappear or appear suddenly. The use of a fog machine to create a murky atmosphere might enhance the graveyard scenes in *Romeo and Juliet*. But such an auditorium stage could also be decorated with just draperies and a few articles of appropriate furniture. A third method of scene setting would be to use a cyclorama and rear projection of such images as clouds, trees, and tombstones.

With a proscenium arch, it is also possible to use a scrim (framed heavy gauge theatrical gauze) for some scenes, allowing for a quick change to the next scene with the mere lifting of the scrim. Having a front curtain means that some scenes—especially those brief scenes of conversation that provide exposition—can be played on the forestage in front of the curtain, and a quick scene change can be effected by the raising of the front curtain to reveal the set behind it.

Taped atmospheric music, sound effects, and lighting effects are easily managed in the conventional proscenium arch auditorium, as there are wings and back stage areas to work from. Such a situation also makes the changing of costumes and the arrangement of a properties table just off stage easily accomplished.

Of course, working on such a large stage has advantages and disadvantages in planning the blocking. There is room to stage sword fights, but there is also the need to "fill the stage" for such events as the Capulets' party and the townspeople rushing to the tomb. If a large cast is not possible, such scenes can be filled by asking the techies to don costumes and swell the processions. Also, when large numbers of actors are on stage together, they often may have to be reminded not to drift into a chorus line arrangement across the stage, but, rather, achieve groupings.

As modern editions of *Romeo and Juliet* divide the play into five acts, you will need to decide on the best place to pause for an intermission or two. More and more plays are being staged with just one intermission; it seems to work best for keeping the audience at the performance until the end. A good place to break *Romeo and Juliet* is after Act 2. This is roughly the middle of the play so each act will be about the same length, but, more importantly, it will end the first act on a high note of romance and danger—all the better to bring the audience back, eager for the second act.

ARENA

In an arena theatre, suggested scenery works best—that is, a group of tree cut-outs, some crafted rocks and boulders, banners, and folding screens. Since there is no front curtain, the scene changes must be effected by the moving on and off of these scenery elements. This can be done by the avista method of having the stagehands in all black clothing working in 20 percent light. It is possible to use scrim at the rear of the fourth area, that not occupied by the audience, but there will not be much depth. It can, however, serve the same purpose as the "inner room" of the Globe's Theatre's rear gallery. Some arena stages are surrounded completely by seating, but it is possible, if you can afford to lose the income from a portion of seats, to block off a fourth of the circle and set up some kind of back-drop.

In such a location a fog machine is not convenient. It should not be used close to an audience; you will have people protesting or coughing as the fog drifts.

Because there are no wings or backstage areas, arena stages usually have provisions for lighting and sound from a booth at the rear or side of the house. Facilities for the props table and any quick costume changes can be arranged behind the blocked off fourth area. Because the audience is so close to the actors, props need to be as realistic looking as possible. In some cases the blocked off area can even be hidden behind a cyclorama, making rear projection possible. Again, because the audience is so close, the sword fighting scenes must be carefully blocked and the actors trained in techniques of stage combat. If this is not possible, productions have achieved good simulations of fighting by using actors in stylized motions on a darkened stage hit with a strobe light.

For asides and other solo speeches, the actors need to be trained to look into the middle distance rather than make eye contact with any audience members.

The suggestion for an intermission given in the section on proscenium arch staging holds good here. And no matter what the location in which the play is staged, it's best to stick to a traditional version of the play. In all likelihood this is the first time the actors will have performed *Romeo and Juliet,* and many in the audience may be seeing the play for the first time. Thus, there is no need to strain for novelty.

FOUND SPACE

When working in an indoor found space, be it cafeteria, classroom, or gymnasium, it's best to use suggested scenery. Unless you intend to rig up a curtain, any scenery changes will need to be effected by the avista method. Since the space is not commonly used for performances, you will need to figure out sightlines for the audience and arrange the seating accordingly. This also affects the blocking of the play. Several configurations may be possible: center staging, horseshoe arrangement of seats, bleachers at the front of your staging area, or dividing the room diagonally.

Lighting can be provided by light trees operated from the rear of the audience. A backdrop or screen at the rear of your playing area can provide a small backstage area for actors and props. The screen must be anchored securely, as young actors making quick exits can easily knock it over.

As the audience is very close to the actors, props and costumes need to be as authentic looking as possible. Even in such close proximity, velveteen and waleless corduroy can look like velvet, and heavy polyester can pass for silk or taffeta. Colors can be used symbolically to add visual interest for the audience since they will not have a handsome set to admire.

As in arena staging, the solo speeches must be delivered to the middle distance and not directly to any audience member. Battle scenes present difficulties, and a director in this situation may elect to keep such action off stage, narrated and further supported by sound effects.

Found spaces usually have built-in distractions: the basketball hoops in the gym, the serving counter in the cafeteria, the bookshelves in the library, the chalkboards in the classroom. Some things can be draped or screened; others kept out of sight by clever lighting plots. Even something as obtrusive as a serving counter in the staging area can be covered and used as a banquet table in *Romeo and Juliet*. There's no discounting the challenge the found space presents, but the rewards for inventiveness are highly enjoyable.

Speaking of challenges, don't be daunted at the prospect of using an outdoor found space. Again, suggested scenery is the best bet, and a fog machine may work well. Light trees can provide adequate lighting, but music and sound effects may be too readily dissipated by the atmosphere and so need to be carefully rehearsed at the exact time of day or night the performances will take place. Then, too, the actors need to get used to projecting their lines in a less than resonant space.

As with the indoor found space, the sightlines will have to be calculated and seating arranged accordingly. If the audience will be seated on a lawn, rather than on chairs, they may be restless and frequently change position. The actors need to realize this and not be disconcerted by it.

The distractions of an outdoor found space range from cars, people, even animals passing by, to insects and unexpected noises. While these may take the attention of the audience for the moment, actors who have been able to rehearse in the space and get used to its problems can win the attention back again.

SELECTED BIBLIOGRAPHY

Beckerman, Bernard. *Shakespeare at the Globe 1599-1609.* New York: Macmillan Co., 1962.

> Covers such topics as the repertory performed at the Globe in that decade, the design of the stage, and the manner in which the plays were staged. Has an appendix with props lists for various Shakespeare productions.

Berman, Ronald. *A Reader's Guide to Shakespeare's Plays.* Glenview, IL: Scott Foresman, 1973.

> Provides a bibliography for each of the plays in such categories as Editions, Sources, Staging, and Criticism.

Bradbrook, M. C. *Themes and Conventions of Elizabethan Tragedy.* Cambridge: Cambridge University Press, 1964.

> The first half of the book deals with conventions of acting, speech, and action. There are references to twenty-four of Shakepeare's plays. The second half contains essays on the major dramatists of the period, such as Marlowe, Webster, and Middleton.

Chambers, E. K. *Shakespeare: A Survey.* New York: Hill and Wang, 1958.

> Containing prefaces to all the plays, it was designed to help the "youthful beginner" approaching Shakespeare for the first time. The language is comprehensible and the tone nonpatronizing. The preface to *Romeo and Juliet* sees the play as a tragedy of lyric emotion, rather than of philosophic insight.

Chute, Marchette. *Shakespeare of London.* New York: E.P. Dutton & Co, Inc., 1949.

> Marchette Chute's portrait of Shakespeare is, as she says, "an attempt to show William Shakespeare as his contemporaries saw him, rather than as the gigantic and legendary figure he has become since." She succeeds in a vivid way, explaining also how certain legends grew up about the bard.

Clemen, Wolfgang. *The Development of Shakespeare's Imagery.* New York: Hill and Wang, 1951.

> Uses thorough examples to show the progressive stages of Shakespeare's imagery. The book is divided into sections on the Early and Middle Periods, and the Romances. There is a long examination of what Clemen calls the "balanced, symmetrical, and artificial style of the early Shakespeare" as seen in *Romeo and Juliet.*

Coghill, Nevill. *Shakespeare's Professional Skills.* Cambridge: Cambridge University Press, 1965.

> In one section Coghill discusses the use Shakespeare made of Arthur Brooke's poem *The Tragicall Historye of Romeus and Juliet* in writing *Romeo and Juliet.*

Dickey, Franklin M. *Not Wisely but Too Well: Shakespeare's Love Tragedies.* San Marino, CA: The Huntington Library, 1957.

> A brief, but scholarly, study of the concept of love in three Shakespearean tragedies—*Romeo and Juliet, Troilus and Cressida,* and *Anthony and Cleopatra.* Dickey finds Shakespeare very much a man of his time in sharing the ethical and religious assumptions of the Elizabethan era.

Doran, Madeleine. *Endeavors of Art: A Study of Elizabethan Drama.* Madison: University of Wisconsin Press, 1964.

> Places the dramatists of the Elizabethan and Jacobean periods in the artistic context of their time. Covers such issues as art vs. nature, Aristotelian rules, and the debt to Roman comedy.

Dyer, T. F. Thiselton. *Folklore of Shakespeare.* New York: Dover, 1966.

> Explores Shakespeare's use of such folkloric elements as fairies, witches, and ghosts, and such elements of nature as birds, plants, and insects. There are also chapters on rituals of baptism, marriage, and burial.

Fluchere, Henri. *Shakespeare and the Elizabethans.* New York: Hill and Wang, 1967.

> Includes a foreword by T.S. Eliot recommending the book for relating Shakespearean drama to the other masterpieces of the Elizabethan theatre. Part One describes the spirit of the Elizabethan age. Part Two deals with techniques of characterization, conventions, and traditions. Part Three explores the major themes and states that in Shakespeare we find the whole of his age. The language is very scholarly.

Harbage, Alfred. *As They Like It: A Study of Shakespeare's Moral Artistry.* Gloucester, MA: Peter Smith, 1971.

> The "they" of the title refers to Shakespeare's original audience which Harbage sees as neither the masses nor a coterie, but rather, a quality audience drawn to a quality playwright at the Globe Theatre. In discussing the enigmas and paradoxes in Shakespeare's plays, Harbage mentions Juliet's father, Romeo and Juliet themselves, and Friar Lawrence.

Holland, Norman N. *The Shakespearean Imagination.* New York: Macmillan Co., 1964.

> The book came from a television course-for-credit developed by Professor Holland for WGBH in Boston. It is written in a lively, good humored manner. The chapter dealing with *Romeo and Juliet* discusses the types of love found within the play—familial, romantic, patriotic, and religious.

Kirschabaum, Leo. *Character and Characterization in Shakespeare.* Detroit: Wayne State University Press, 1962.

> There are ten essays, each on a Shakespearean character. In the chapter on Romeo, the author seeks to disprove the charge that Romeo is fickle by placing him well within the convention of the Elizabethan young man of fashion.

Robinson, Randal. *Unlocking Shakespeare's Language: Help for the Teacher and Student.* Urbana, IL: National Council of Teachers of English and the ERIC Clearinghouse on Reading and Communication Skills, 1989.

Especially prepared for secondary and undergraduate college teachers, this publication addresses the problems most often encountered by beginning students of Shakespeare. Robinson draws on the contemporary and the colloquial to help students unravel such Shakespearean structures as inverted sentences, delayed constructions, and separations of related parts. Worksheets are included.

Spurgeon, Caroline. *Shakespeare's Imagery and What it Tells Us.* Cambridge: Cambridge University Press, 1968.

Examines dominant images in Shakespeare in order to comment on the characters and themes of his plays. Some image clusters considered are those drawn from astronomy, sports, the sea, birds, food, medicine, and music.

Styan, J. L. *Shakespeare's Stagecraft.* Cambridge: Cambridge University Press, 1967.

Filled with interesting details of Shakespeare's stage and the acting conventions of his time, this volume also offers suggestions for blocking the plays on stage. In one of the sections on *Romeo and Juliet,* some of the play's comic relief is explored.

APPENDICES AND GLOSSARY

Following are two appendices that you will wish to duplicate for your students. The Guide to Pronouncing Proper Names in *Romeo and Juliet* should probably be given to students at the beginning of the study of this play. (The terms in this guide are taken from the translation.) The same would hold true for the Shakespearean Time Line. It is useful to be reminded of the events of Shakespeare's life and how they fit into an overall historical framework. A third appendix contains an excerpt from Shakespeare's source.

The items in the Glossary are arranged alphabetically, and references are given in parentheses to their use in the play.

APPENDIX I:

A GUIDE TO PRONOUNCING PROPER NAMES
IN *ROMEO AND JULIET*

Aurora	ä-RŌ-rŭ
Baltasar	băl-TÄ-zär *or* băl-THÄ-zär
Benvolio	bĕn-VŌ-lĭ-o *or* bĕn-VŌ-leo
Capulet	KĂP-ū-lĕt
Cleopatra	klē-ō-PĀ-trŭ *or* klā-ō-PĂT-rŭ
Cupid	KIŪ-pĭd
Diana	dī-ĂN-ŭ
Dido	DĪ-dō
Escalus	ĔS-kŭ-lŭs
Friar Lawrence	FRĪ-er LŌ-rĕns
Gregory	GRĔG-ō-rĭ *or* GRĔG-rĭ
Helen	HĔL-ĕn
Hero	HĒ-rō
Juliet	JĪŪL-yĕt *or* JIŪ-lĭ-ĕt
Lammastide	LĂM-ŭs-TĪD
Laura	LŌ-rŭ
Mantua	MĂN-choo-ŭ *or* MĂN-tiu-ŭ

Mercutio	mĕr-KĪU-shĭō
Montague	MŎN-tĭ-gīu
Paris	PĂ-ris
Petrarch	PĒ-trärk
Phaeton	FĀ-ĕ-thŭn *or* FĀ-ĕ-tŭn
Phoebus	FĒ-bŭs
Romeo	RŌ-mēō
Sampson	SĂMP-sŭn
Thisbe	THĬZ-bē
Tybalt	TĬB-ŭlt
Verona	vĕ-RŌ-nŭ

KEY: āce, ärm, ăt, ēve, mĕt, īce, hĭt, ōld, ŏx, ūse, ŭp

APPENDIX II:
SHAKESPEAREAN TIME LINE

1557
Marriage of John Shakespeare of Stratford-upon-Avon to Mary Arden

1558
Accession of Queen Elizabeth

1564
Christening of William Shakespeare, third child of John and Mary Shakespeare

1568
John Shakespeare becomes bailiff, or mayor, of Stratford

1576
First permanent theatre built in London

1577-80
John Shakespeare experiences financial difficulties

1582
Marriage of William Shakespeare and Anne Hathaway

1583
Christening of Susanna, daughter of William and Anne Shakespeare, at Holy Trinity Church in Stratford

1585
Christening of Hamnet and Judith, twin children of Anne and William Shakespeare, at Holy Trinity Church in Stratford

1588
Defeat of the Spanish Armada sent to invade England

1592
Shakespeare mentioned as an actor and a playwright by Robert Greene. London theatres closed because of the plague

1593
Shakespeare publishes *Venus and Adonis*, a long narrative poem, based on poems by Ovid, and dedicated to his patron the Earl of Southampton

1594
London theatres reopened
Shakespeare becomes a member and a shareholder in the Lord Chamberlain's company of actors

1596
Hamnet Shakespeare dies

1597
Shakespeare purchases New Place, one of the largest houses in Stratford

1598
Francis Meres mentions "honey-tongued" Shakespeare as the author of twelve successful plays

1599
The Globe Theater built and opened by Shakespeare's company

1601
John Shakespeare dies

1603
Queen Elizabeth dies, and James I ascends the throne
The Chamberlain's Men become the King's Men

1609
The Blackfriars Theatre taken over by the King's Men in addition to the Globe

1610
Probable retirement of Shakespeare to Stratford

1616
Shakespeare dies at Stratford

1623
Publication of Shakespeare's collected plays, the First Folio

APPENDIX III:
A BRIEF LOOK AT SHAKESPEARE'S SOURCE

The immediate source for Shakespeare's play was Arthur Brooke's poem *The Tragicall Historye of Romeus and Juliet* (1562). Here is the conclusion of that poem. The spelling has been modernized, but archaic words such as *eke* ("also") and *ne* ("not") have been preserved. You might have your students compare this excerpt with the ending of Shakespeare's play. Have them compare similarities and note differences. Ask them to speculate on the differences.

> The wiser sort to counsel called by Escalus,
> Have given advice, and Escalus sagely decreeth thus.
> The nurse of Juliet, is banished in her age,
> Because that from the parents she did hide the marriage,
> Which might have wrought much good, had it in time been known,
> Where now by her concealing it, a mischief great is grown;
>
> . . . .
>
> Th'apothecary, high is hanged by the throat,
> And for the pains he took with him, the hangman had his coat.
> But now what shall betide of this gray-bearded sire?
> Of friar Lawrence thus arraigned, that good barefooted friar?
> Because that many times he worthily did serve
> The commonwealth, and in his life was never found to swerve,
> He was discharged quite, and no mark of defame
> Did seem to blot, or touch at all, the honor of his name.
> But of himself he went into an Hermitage,
> Two miles from Verona town, where he in prayers passed forth his age.
> Till that from earth to heaven, his heavenly spirit did fly.
> Five years he lived an Hermit, and an Hermit did he die.
> The strangeness of the chance, when tried was the truth
> The Montagues and Capulets have moved so to ruth,
> That with their emptied tears, their choler and their rage,
> Was emptied quite, and they whose wrath no wisdom could assuage,
> Nor threat'ning of the prince, ne mind of murders done,
> At length, (so mighty Jove it would) by pity they are won.
>
> And lest that length of time might from our minds remove
> The memory of so perfect, sound, and so approved love,
> The bodies dead removed from vault where they did die,
> In stately tomb, on pillars great, of marble raise they high.
> On every side above, were set and eke beneath,

Great store of cunning Epitaphs, in honor of their death.
And even at this day the tomb is to be seen,
So that among the monuments that in Verona been,
There is no monument more worthy of the sight,
Than is the tomb of Juliet, and Romeus her knight.

GLOSSARY

The following terms are taken from this translation of *The Tragedy of Romeo and Juliet*. Act, scene, and line numbers are given in parentheses after the terms.

Benedicite (act 2, scene 3, line 33): Latin for "God bless you"

cockatrice (act 3, scene 2, line 49): a legendary serpent with the head, wings, and feet of a cock, able to kill with its look

Cupid (act 1, scene 1, line 207): god of love. He is often pictured as a child, blindfolded, carrying a bow and arrows

Diana (act 1, scene 1, line 207): the moon goddess, who chose to remain a virgin

Dido...Cleopatra...Helen...Hero...Thisbe (act 2, scene 4, lines 37-39): romantic heroines of legend

Echo (act 2, scene 2, line 170): nymph whose unrequited love for Narcissus caused her to waste away until nothing was left but her voice. She lived in caves and could only repeat what others said

"Heart's Ease" (act 4, scene 5, line 104): a popular song during Shakespeare's time

Lammastide (act 1, scene 3, line 17): a religious festival, beginning August 1, giving thanks for the harvest by blessing loaves of bread made from the new crop

Lent (act 2, scene 4, line 117): a season of fasting and penitence, ending the day before Easter

mandrakes (act 4, scene 3, line 49): plants whose forked roots resemble human figures. They were thought to shriek when pulled from the earth, and anyone hearing the sound supposedly went mad

Mantua (act 1, scene 3, line 31): a town in northern Italy, about 25 miles from Verona

palmers (act 1, scene 5, line 104): religious pilgrims who carried palm branches to show they had visited the Holy Land

Pentecost (act 1, scene 5, line 36): a religious feast occurring fifty days after Easter, celebrating the descent of the Holy Spirit upon the apostles of Christ

Petrarch (act 2, scene 4, line 36): fourteenth-century Italian poet who wrote sonnets to an idealized woman, Laura

Phaeton (act 3, scene 2, line 3): the son of Phoebus Apollo who was allowed to drive his father's chariot for one day, lost control, and was destroyed by a thunderbolt from Jupiter

pinked shoe (act 2, scene 4, line 55): a shoe with small decorative holes

plantain leaf (act 1, scene 2, line 52): broad leaf used to staunch the flow of blood

Prince of Cats (act 2, scene 4, line 18): a play on Tybalt's name, which is close to that of Sir Tybert, the Prince of Cats in the medieval fable *Reynard the Fox*

Queen Mab (act 1, scene 4, line 57): this mythological creature has no known earlier reference, so she may be Shakespeare's invention

re, fa (act 4, scene 5, line 118): the second and fourth notes of the musical scale

rebeck (act 4, scene 5, line 131): a stringed instrument, ancestor of the violin

star-crossed (Prologue, line 6): born under the unfavorable influence of the stars and destined for unhappiness

Tally ho! (act 2, scene 4, line 115): the call of a hunter at the sight of a fox

Venus (act 2, scene 1, line 13): goddess of love and beauty

Verona (Prologue, line 2): a town in northeastern Italy